Praise for *The Power Formula fo...*

"Social networks are evolving into commercial networl work—and thus are an increasingly important cha points out in his excellent book, LinkedIn is all abou ...e right connections, which is why we view it as an invaluable tool for recruiting talent that helps our clients win. Buy at least 396 copies of Wayne's book and share it with all your friends."
—Mark Toth, chief legal officer, Manpower North America

"I know of no one who knows how to use LinkedIn better than Wayne Breitbarth. That he is willing to share his knowledge so clearly and concisely is truly a gift—his gift to anyone who needs to connect for business, for fun, or to find a job."
—Robert Grede, bestselling author of *Naked Marketing* and *The Spur & The Sash*

"I own a small business and have followed Wayne's advice to better utilize LinkedIn. By revising my profile, participating in groups, and more effectively using the advanced search function, I've been able to get connected to key decision-makers and drive traffic to our website. It's been a great business development tool for my company."
—Jeff Carrigan, founder and CMO, Big Shoes Network

"*The Power Formula* greatly simplifies the ability of those of us not in the Facebook generation to make sense of social media and leverage LinkedIn for business success."
—Michael A. Dalton, author of *Simplifying Innovation*

"This book is just like Wayne himself—smart, down-to-earth, and full of good ideas. *The Power Formula for LinkedIn Success* explains how anyone can use LinkedIn to propel business growth. With clear explanations and real-life examples, it's a must-read for anyone who is serious about business development."
—Christina Steder, president, Clear Verve Marketing

"While college students are not strangers to social media, having direction and focus on how to appropriately and professionally use LinkedIn as a tool for researching careers and networking with professionals is essential. Wayne Breitbarth gives great instruction for this tech-savvy yet new-to-the-workforce population."
—Laura F. Kestner, director, Career Services Center, Marquette University

"The combination of Wayne Breitbarth's passion for the power of social networking and his real-world business experience, deep knowledge, mastery of LinkedIn, and skill as a trainer make the *The Power Formula for LinkedIn Success* a real standout. This is the one book to buy if you are serious about getting up to speed fast."
—Frank Martinelli, president, The Center for Public Skills Training

"Wayne's delightful book will help you build competence in understanding LinkedIn, gain confidence in using this important tool, and enable you to take the risk of embracing social media to advance your professional goals. Buy it today!"

—Susan Marshall, president, Executive Advisor LLC, and author of *How to Grow a Backbone*

"Wayne Breitbarth unlocks the secrets to successfully using one of the most important business tools in today's arsenal: LinkedIn. *The Power Formula for LinkedIn Success* is a practical tool for anyone looking to significantly improve their career, business, or professional standing. Breitbarth's Power Formula provides a simple and easy-to-use method for increasing visibility through one of today's most popular digital platforms. His down-to-earth writing style, combined with loads of LinkedIn insights, makes this a must-have book for anyone not wanting to get passed by on today's digital business superhighway."

—Rich Horwath, author of *Deep Dive: The Proven Method for Building Strategy, Focusing Your Resources, and Taking Smart Action*

"If you've asked 'Where's the value of LinkedIn?' or 'Why should I invest the time to use LinkedIn?', then you need to read Wayne's book! His Power Formula provides brilliant insight and guidance on how to get started using the LinkedIn platform to get your arms around the most powerful asset you have—your network of relationships. Whether you are averse to technology, or an executive with little time to spare, Wayne will show you where the value is!"

—Michael Kuhlman, president, 123Smarket.com

The Power Formula for

LinkedIn

Success

The Power Formula for

LinkedIn

Success

Kick-start Your Business, Brand, *and* Job Search

Wayne Breitbarth

GREENLEAF
BOOK GROUP PRESS

Published by Greenleaf Book Group Press
Austin, Texas
www.gbgpress.com

Copyright ©2019 Wayne Breitbarth

All rights reserved.

Thank you for purchasing an authorized edition of this book and for complying with copyright law. No part of this book may be reproduced, stored in a retrieval system, or transmitted by any means, electronic, mechanical, photocopying, recording, or otherwise, without written permission from the copyright holder.

Distributed by Greenleaf Book Group

For ordering information or special discounts for bulk purchases, please contact Greenleaf Book Group at PO Box 91869, Austin, TX 78709, 512.891.6100.

Design and composition by Greenleaf Book Group and Publications Development Company
Cover design by Greenleaf Book Group

Publisher's Cataloging-in-Publication data is available.
Print ISBN: 978-1-62634-620-8
eBook ISBN: 978-1-62634-621-5

Part of the Tree Neutral® program, which offsets the number of trees consumed in the production and printing of this book by taking proactive steps, such as planting trees in direct proportion to the number of trees used: www.treeneutral.com

TreeNeutral

Printed in the United States of America on acid-free paper

19 20 21 22 23 24   10 9 8 7 6 5 4 3 2 1

Fourth Edition

Contents

Resources

Bonus Online Resources

The Definitive Worksheet to Optimize Your
LinkedIn Profile Headline
www.powerformula.net/free

The LinkedIn Connection Conundrum: Who Should
Be in Your Network?
www.powerformula.net/connections

10 LinkedIn Mistakes Companies Make—and How to Fix
Them Before They Damage Your Company's Reputation
www.powerformula.net/mistakes

Should You Hide Your LinkedIn Connections?
www.powerformula.net/hideconnections

About This Book

This book is meant to help you quickly, efficiently, and pain-lessly discover whether this thing called LinkedIn is worth your time and effort and to understand how to effectively use it to accomplish your business goals. You may choose to read it cover to cover or immediately begin applying the techniques and strategies discussed in each chapter. In either case, it will be an important reference as you move from novice to experienced user. I sincerely hope you will find this book to be motivational, educational, and entertaining.

Also provided in this book are links to a variety of valuable resources to further assist you in using LinkedIn to successfully brand and market yourself and your business.

Most of the step-by-step instructions in this book relate to the desktop version of LinkedIn, but the overall strategies, in most instances, apply to desktop and mobile. However, Chapter 14 is devoted solely to the LinkedIn mobile app, and you'll find lots of tips and tricks for making the most of LinkedIn while on the go.

As with most Internet-based resources, there will be periodic updates and other changes to the LinkedIn website and mobile app. In order for this book to remain relevant and accurate, I will periodically address these modifications. Visit my website at www.powerformula.net, and sign up to receive these important notifications and/or register to receive free weekly LinkedIn tips.

Introduction

I Never Even Wanted to Be on LinkedIn!

I never wanted to be on LinkedIn, never thought it would be useful, and surely never wanted to spend a significant amount of time teaching other business executives how to use it. I am not someone who loves technology for technology's sake; I am an experienced businessperson who respects the experience and knowledge of other businesspeople. Business professionals tend to be interested in thoroughly exploring the "why" before launching into the "how to." Thus, this book is designed to not only teach you how to effectively use LinkedIn but also to show you why the tools, techniques, and strategies presented here can be instrumental in furthering your professional goals. With that in mind, let me share with you some background on my LinkedIn journey and explain why I think LinkedIn is an important tool for you to investigate and master.

Think back to the time you received your very first e-mail. If you were like me, you looked at that e-mail and said, "Nah, this will never work. People will never communicate this way, and I'm sure if I ignore this, it will just go away." Well, do you know anyone today who doesn't have an e-mail account? Can you even imagine going a day (or perhaps even a couple of hours) without checking your e-mail?

In my opinion, the whole social media phenomenon, and LinkedIn in particular, has that same kind of feel to it. Although I am not a futurist, it's clear that the process of connecting with people over the Internet is here to stay. When people attend my training classes, especially people in my age group (as of this writing, I am sixty years old), many of them hope the ninety minutes they spend will confirm their suspicion that this tool is worthless or avoidable. It may be your secret desire (or maybe your not-so-secret desire) that when you finish this book, you'll be able to confidently say, "Great. No value there. Now I can move on. My life is too busy for LinkedIn anyway!"

That is why I approach my training classes as well as this book with the intention of not necessarily teaching you every specific technique of using LinkedIn but instead showing you its capabilities so that you can get rid of the fear factor. I suspect that fear comes from two sources: Potential users ask themselves, "What will happen if I jump into the murky waters of LinkedIn?" or, more importantly, "Will I be at a competitive disadvantage if my competitors embrace this technology while I sit on the fence?"

My goal is for you to end up in one of three camps after reading this book. First, you may gain an understanding of the concept and recognize what you might be missing but choose instead to spend your time finding another way to brand or market yourself and your business. That's fine. LinkedIn isn't necessarily for everyone. Second, once you have a better understanding of the capabilities of LinkedIn, you may decide to either tinker with it on a limited basis or strategize about how you may be able to use it to advance your career or business in a few key ways. Or, third, you may decide this is a rockin' tool and realize you'd better get on board completely—and also have people in your company fully understand its concepts, premises, and working parts.

LinkedIn is all about using the Internet to find and be found by people—in addition to using the good old-fashioned face-to-face method of meeting people. Perhaps over time more personal contact will be replaced with virtual interactions, but LinkedIn will never completely take the place of meeting people in your business sphere and spending time with them, either on the phone or in person. People still prefer to do business with people they know and trust, and typically knowing and trusting takes place much more rapidly when contact occurs on a face-to-face basis.

None of us is looking for another thing to do for two or three hours each week to replace spending time with our families, playing golf, fishing, or engaging in other hobbies we enjoy. Therefore, my hope is that the time you spend on LinkedIn will not necessarily add a burden to your already busy life but that it will allow you to do a form of networking 24/7, perhaps while watching your favorite TV shows or sporting events. Being a Wisconsinite, it is my duty to watch the Green Bay Packers play football on TV each Sunday afternoon. However, I have within me this nagging little voice that says, *Wayne, this is not a very productive endeavor*, especially when the Packers are getting annihilated. Now, with the help of my laptop, tablet, or smartphone, LinkedIn allows me to keep track of what is going on in my network of professionals, while at the same time keeping an eye on the Packers game.

LinkedIn is the world's largest online business networking site. You join LinkedIn either by going to LinkedIn.com and setting up an account or by accepting an invitation from someone who has suggested you sign up. Most people are invited by several friends or business associates before making the decision to join LinkedIn, and it usually takes an invitation from a very trusted friend before they get started. However, even after they take the first step, it's common for people to not really know what or why they are joining; they simply check the box and begin the journey without either knowing what LinkedIn does or having a strategy for how to use it.

By the time this book hits the shelves, LinkedIn will have over half a billion users, with two new members being added every second of the day. Approximately 28 percent of those members are in the United States. The following chart enumerates some interesting statistics relating to the demographics of LinkedIn users:

THE LINKEDIN PROFESSIONAL AT A GLANCE

Over age 30	63%
Male/Female	54% / 46%
Some College/College Grad	74%
Household Income $75K+	45%

Source: Pew Research Center (January 2017)

Here's how I got started on LinkedIn. I have a very close friend who nagged me Sunday after Sunday at church, explaining that I should get on LinkedIn, and I consistently blew him off, saying, "I don't have time to keep track of your LinkedIn or Plaxo or Facebook or any other website." Yet he consistently said to me, "Listen—you are a small business owner and you really need this."

Well, as luck would have it, one afternoon I found myself stuck in a hotel room in a remote location with nothing to do. It's not my style to spend the afternoon watching TV, so I thought I would check out this LinkedIn thing and see what it was about. Two hours later, I had overcome my fear and ordered two books about LinkedIn from Amazon.com. I now saw LinkedIn as a powerful tool and wanted to become an expert as soon as humanly possible. Four or five hours later, in that same hotel room, I was en route to becoming a passionate proponent of virtual networking. I immediately began connecting with people from my past, including college classmates and employees of many of the companies I had worked with in the Milwaukee area over the previous thirty years.

In response to my newfound enthusiasm, friends and colleagues began asking me questions about LinkedIn. After admitting I had become a LinkedIn junkie, I would invite them into our company's boardroom (I owned an office furniture dealership at the time) and spend time sharing what I knew about LinkedIn with them. This turned into a formal class, followed by requests from local chambers of commerce, Rotary clubs, etc. to educate their members about the far-reaching benefits of LinkedIn. And as they say, the rest is history. More than 80,000 people have read the first, second, and third editions of this book, and you are reading the fourth edition. I am now a nationally recognized speaker, and I consult with companies across the country, helping them use LinkedIn to promote their products and services and increase their revenue.

Despite the fact that LinkedIn is often referred to as "Facebook for businesspeople," what businesspeople appreciate and respect about LinkedIn is that it has significant processes and controls that keep it from becoming like Facebook. At the time of this writing, Facebook has over two billion members, and the ability to connect with such a vast number of people certainly does attract some businesspeople. However, many facets of Facebook—such as pictures of your past tagged with your name (and possibly including beer bongs and bikinis), relationship statuses, and religious and political views—are things that totally turn off most businesspeople to using the site for professional networking. Facebook does have significant applications for businesses (especially those that sell directly to consumers), but many businesspeople feel more comfortable with LinkedIn because of its built-in controls and personal settings. I will discuss many of those controls and settings in subsequent chapters of this book.

By now you are, no doubt, anxious to get started. So fasten your seat belt and prepare to see your fear subside as you learn more about what LinkedIn is and how it can help you kick-start your business, brand, and job search.

CHAPTER 1

A New Way to
Look at Social Media
The LinkedIn Power Formula

I had been on LinkedIn for just over a year and had taught more than 120 classes, with over four thousand participants, when I had a revelation: All of these social media tools are just that—tools! No different than a hammer, which is only as good as the person swinging it. As I started to think about this more and more, I realized that there is one group of people—we will call them the Facebook generation—and then there are the rest of us, the non-Facebook generations. The first group is darned good at social media and grasp it so much more easily than we do, since they grew up with the Internet. They embrace new social technologies in a big hurry, which scares the heck out of many of us in the non-Facebook group. So, instead of deciding we should get on board, we just hope it will go away, thinking that maybe we'll wake up one day, it will all be gone, and things will be back to "normal."

I'm not telling you this because I want to bring you down even further but because I have some good news about the person swinging the hammer: you. You already have lots of experience and relationships that you can leverage to make your use of LinkedIn—or any other social media site—much more effective. It is this revelation that helped me come up with the idea of the Power Formula:

Your Unique Experience + Your Unique Relationships + The Tool (in this case, LinkedIn) = The Power

Anyone with business experience and the willingness to learn can realize great benefits from LinkedIn. And getting started with LinkedIn is really not that big of a deal. You can either read a book about how to use LinkedIn, attend a seminar, consult an expert you trust, or check out the Help Center on LinkedIn.com. Learn as much as you can, and then take the time to execute the strategies you have been shown. Make the commitment to get this done, and make it a priority to establish some good LinkedIn habits. No matter how tech-savvy they are, members of the Facebook generation cannot go to a two-hour seminar and come away with the wealth of experience and relationships that comes from years of meetings, handshakes, small talk, weekend retreats, planning sessions, bad proposals, good proposals, winning jobs, losing jobs, etc. But members of the non-Facebook generations, who have the benefit of these experiences and relationships, can be right where they want to be after just one weekend and an ongoing commitment to a LinkedIn strategy. That's how I started ten years ago. I got on LinkedIn.com, bought a few books, digested the information, and was on my way to creating my own LinkedIn strategy.

Let me address the components of the Power Formula in greater detail so you can better grasp its importance.

Your Unique Experience

Every one of us has unique experiences that we bring to the marketplace. These experiences come from our education, jobs, culture, ethnicity, interests, and family, to name a few. Today, with virtual marketing and promotion more important than ever, developing a strong personal brand is essential, and your unique experience is a substantial component of that brand. The longer you have been in the marketplace, the more experiences you have amassed, each of which may come to bear on your next business opportunity.

Your Unique Relationships

Because none of us has walked the same path or encountered the same people, we have each developed a unique set of relationships. These relationships have been the foundation of our friendships, business partnerships, and customer bases. When we need help, whether personally or professionally, we turn to these people— our network. They in turn know that we are just a phone call away when we have the knowledge, experience, or resources to assist them. Our networks are one of our most valuable possessions, and as they continue to expand and diversify, they become even more important to our business and personal lives.

The Tool

The tool could be anything that helps accelerate or "power up" your ability to accomplish your goals, and social media tools certainly fall into this category. Traditionally, when the old tool is "working just fine," we can be reluctant to embrace the new tool, despite its promise to be better, faster, or perhaps even cheaper. For instance, your old, paper address book (the tool) worked just fine, but you eventually made the switch to a new tool—perhaps Microsoft Outlook. The process of learning to use the new tool may have been challenging at first, but your commitment and persistence were rewarded when you finally figured out how to retrieve all that valuable information with the click of a button.

So, why did I take all this time to share with you my revelation about the Power Formula when I told you I would be teaching you about the capabilities and functions of LinkedIn? Because I want you to understand that the **unique experience** you have gained coupled with the **unique relationships** you have carefully developed gives you a tremendous advantage over the person who understands **the tool** (in this case, LinkedIn) but is only beginning to gain experience and develop professional relationships.

Am I trying to discourage those of you who are younger business professionals or just starting your business careers? No way! This book will help you understand how to begin to develop your personal brand by creating a compelling LinkedIn profile and expanding your network in order to accomplish your professional goals.

To help you keep focused on the Power Formula as you read this book, there will be a box at the end of each chapter that reemphasizes key points in terms of your **unique experience** and **unique relationships**. These sections will help you define your own power formula for succeeding in whatever you hope to accomplish in your career.

CHAPTER 2

The Million-Workstation Project
LinkedIn—Making the Invisible Visible

LinkedIn has described their mission as follows: "Connect the world's professionals to make them more productive and successful. When you join LinkedIn, you get access to people, jobs, news, updates, and insights that help you be great at what you do." Let me start by addressing how LinkedIn works from a practical standpoint.

In their current user agreement, LinkedIn states, "You agree that you will not invite people you do not know to join your network." In earlier versions of the user agreement, they referred to "your network of trusted professionals." They are obviously encouraging their members to only connect with people they know. This is where LinkedIn differs significantly from social media sites like Facebook, where members attempt to get as many "friends" as they can—and where the word *friend* is loosely defined. With LinkedIn, the goal is to connect with only those people whom you consider to be trusted professionals. That leads to the first strategic decision you have to make: You need to personally decide whom you will consider a trusted professional based on the strategy you intend to pursue on LinkedIn. Some people choose to focus on expanding their networks even if this means embracing a loose definition of the word *trusted*. In contrast, I like to say a person is trusted if I can pick up the phone and ask him for a favor or an introduction and be confident that he would say "yes," or if he is someone for whom I would do the same.

The person you just met in the vegetable aisle at your local grocery store typically does not meet my standard of a trusted professional. He might be a nice person and you may have enjoyed the two minutes of conversation, but that doesn't qualify him as "trusted" when he runs home and decides to look for you on LinkedIn. The decision about who is "trusted" is a very important starting point with LinkedIn, and there are lots of debates about this matter. However, in my opinion, most LinkedIn users will be best served by following a more conservative definition of trusted. I will provide additional comments and thoughts later on the always-raging debate between quality and quantity as it relates to your network.

Once you have opened a LinkedIn account and begun connecting with your trusted friends and colleagues, your database on LinkedIn begins to grow in ways that are obvious (your number of connections gets larger) but also in ways that are not so obvious. In order to truly comprehend the power of LinkedIn, it is important to understand the part you cannot see—your extended network.

LinkedIn is constantly evolving, and the information shown in Figure 2.1 is no longer available on the LinkedIn site in this form, but I include it here to help you visualize degrees of separation—the Kevin Bacon concept that we are all connected by six degrees of separation or less to virtually everyone in the world. You will notice here that there are three circled numbers: 1, 2, and 3. The first group is one degree away from you; these are your personal connections, labeled with the subheading "Your trusted friends and colleagues."

Figure 2.1: LinkedIn makes your extended network visible.

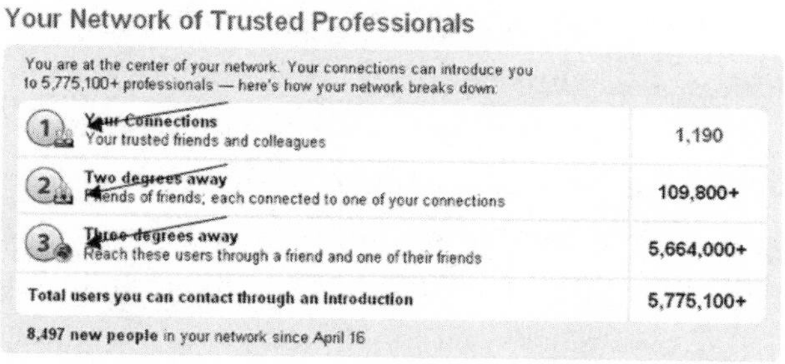

Your Network of Trusted Professionals

You are at the center of your network. Your connections can introduce you to 5,775,100+ professionals — here's how your network breaks down:

1 Your Connections Your trusted friends and colleagues	1,190
2 Two degrees away Friends of friends; each connected to one of your connections	109,800+
3 Three degrees away Reach these users through a friend and one of their friends	5,664,000+
Total users you can contact through an introduction	5,775,100+

8,497 new people in your network since April 16

Here is an example of how first-degree connections work. Let's say I have a friend named Joe Smith. Joe and I have been friends for a long time. Maybe we hung out in the rain at our kids' soccer games or perhaps we are close business associates. I decide that Joe and I should connect on LinkedIn. I search for his name, find him, and extend an invitation to Joe, asking him to join my LinkedIn network. Once Joe accepts my invitation, he does not need to turn around and invite me into his network as well. At that point, we are both connected to each other at the first level.

Your first-degree connections should be people who are already part of your offline network. You have a network that you have built over the course of your lifetime, whether that be high school, college, places you worked, clubs to which you belong, or from connections through your day-to-day life. This is what I call your "flat" network. The premise of LinkedIn is that you transform your "flat" list of contacts into a dynamic, multidimensional network. Putting your contacts into LinkedIn will enable you to access additional degrees of depth within your network and will allow your contacts to assist you in new and valuable ways.

Let's go back to Joe Smith, my first-degree connection. When I owned an office furniture dealership, if Joe were building a building and needed my products and services, he would probably call me because I know him so well. The fun begins when you think about the second degree. Let's say Joe Smith knows Bob Anderson. I have never met Bob Anderson. However, let's say that Bob is going to build a new building in town, and rumor has it that this building will contain over a million workstations. As a furniture guy, a million-workstation job in a town the size of mine would be a *really* big deal. Your equivalent of my million-workstation sale might be finding the perfect job, meeting a strategic partner who will bring you additional revenue, finding a vendor that will enable you to decrease your production costs, or connecting with a foundation or individual who is interested in assisting your favorite charity.

Let's say I hear that Bob's company, The Anderson Company, is going to construct this building, and I put either "Bob Anderson" or "The Anderson Company" into the LinkedIn search engine and find out that my friend Joe Smith is connected to Bob Anderson. I find this out because when I do a search, I see that Bob's name is followed by a "2nd" icon, which means he knows one of my first-degree connections. I may know some of Joe's friends—having golfed, gone to parties, or hung out with many of them—but I definitely don't know all of them. For this example, let's assume I do not know Bob and do not know how he knows my friend Joe.

So, learning of this connection after searching LinkedIn, I excitedly call Joe and ask him if he would connect me with his friend Bob Anderson, to which he replies, "Are you kidding? Of course. He's a good friend of mine. We've been friends for a long, long time. If my connecting you with Bob can help you, I'd love to do it." Isn't that what networks have always done? The added benefit of LinkedIn is that I can now see a list of Joe's connections and request an introduction to any of his connections I would like to meet.

Stop and think about the power of that. Without LinkedIn, what are the chances I would know that Joe Smith knows Bob Anderson? But with this tool, I can find it out almost immediately and can then use my network to connect with Bob.

Let's take it one step further, to the third degree, and imagine that Bob Anderson is friends with Jill Jones. Remember that I don't know Bob or Jill—I only know Joe. However, I now have the ability to search Jill Jones and The Jones Company, only to find out that Jill is building a building with—you guessed it—a million workstations. I now have a chance to talk with her by contacting Joe, who contacts Bob, who contacts Jill.

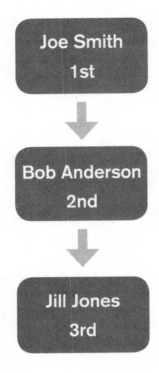

Let's just take a look at the total number of people I had access to through LinkedIn at the time I captured this screenshot (see Figure 2.2). Joe is a first-degree connection, Bob is a second-degree connection, and Jill is a third-degree connection, and I had 1,190 Joes, 109,800 Bobs, and over 5.6 million people in the Jill Jones category. These numbers never cease to amaze me. Sometimes I think there must be some dogs and cats in those numbers—there's no way I could be connected to that many businesspeople. However, at this point I actually did have over 5.7 million human connections (no cats or dogs!), many of whom may have led me to that million-workstation sale. I always had over 5.7 million people in my extended network; I just never knew who they were and how they were connected to me. And my network has grown exponentially since this point.

Figure 2.2: Your network grows exponentially.

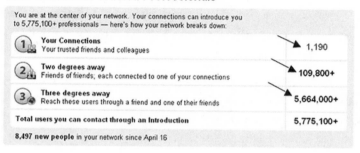

Your Network of Trusted Professionals

You are at the center of your network. Your connections can introduce you to 5,775,100+ professionals — here's how your network breaks down:

① **Your Connections** Your trusted friends and colleagues	▲ 1,190
② **Two degrees away** Friends of friends; each connected to one of your connections	▲ 109,800+
③ **Three degrees away** Reach these users through a friend and one of their friends	▲ 5,664,000+
Total users you can contact through an Introduction	5,775,100+

8,497 new people in your network since April 16

Remember the good old-fashioned method of networking? If I wanted to get ahold of either Bob Anderson or Jill Jones to talk about a potential business opportunity, I would be calling them (if I even knew their names) and sending e-mails, letters, postcards, whatever. The other thirteen furniture dealers who are located in my town would undoubtedly be using the same tactics. This would probably result in Bob and Jill screaming, "No more furniture guys!" With LinkedIn, I can have a friend or a friend of a friend assist me in making a contact that would typically be extremely difficult to coordinate. This is the number one power of LinkedIn: It takes connections that would normally be invisible and makes them visible.

Now let me give you an example of what could happen if you and your contacts choose to embrace the strategy of using a more casual definition of the word *trusted*. Say I am very excited about the opportunity of a workstation sale because when I searched Bob Anderson and his company, I found that he is a second-degree connection. I call my first-degree connection, Joe Smith, and Joe says, "I don't think I know him. Who is Bob?"

"Bob Anderson," I say. "He is connected to you on LinkedIn. Of course you know him."

"Wayne, I really don't know him."

"You've got to be kidding me. He's a first-degree connection with you on LinkedIn. I can see it. How can you not know somebody in your network?"

If that happens several times, I might say to Joe, "Your network stinks. You really don't know anybody you're connected to. You just have a whole bunch of names in there, and you don't have any deep relationships with anyone. You're like a kid on Facebook."

That's why I stick with the premise that for most people, your network should be made up of people you know and trust; it allows you to help people. When you get to three degrees away, you hope the relationship that exists between yourself and your first-degree connection is as strong as the first to the second and the second to the third. If not, the connective power of LinkedIn can be greatly diminished.

The majority of books and blogs on the subject of networking say most business professionals have between 200 and 250 people they consider trusted professionals. If you're not on LinkedIn, these contacts are probably kept and managed in some kind of document or file, such as a Microsoft Outlook file on your computer, a card file, a list of names of people, a box of business cards in the top drawer of your desk, etc. All I am asking you to consider doing is taking those 200 to 250 contacts and getting them into LinkedIn. That way, you will not only have those 200 to 250 first-degree contacts; you will also gain the ability to know who their first-degree connections and their second-degree connections are. Your contacts' first-degree connections and second-degree connections then become your second-degree connections and third-degree connections. At this point, the number of people in your

LinkedIn network can get incredibly large, as you saw in the previous example.

Let me stop and ask you this question: Can you have too many first-degree connections? If you answered yes, you are mostly correct. But let me ask the question differently: Can you have too many first-degree connections as long as each one is trusted? The answer is no—as long as they are trusted, you cannot have too many first-degree connections, and you shouldn't second-guess the potential significance of what that first-degree connection does, where he lives, or what his background is. That is not the point. As long as he fits your criterion of being trusted, make him a first-degree connection so that you can find out whom he is connected to—and potentially connect with all of his connections and his connections' connections. You have no idea who she plays golf with every Saturday or who he sat next to in church last Sunday.

In the past few years, I have read countless books, blogs, and commentaries about LinkedIn, and the quality versus quantity issue is continually debated by authors. This is the question of whether it's better to have a huge network of people you do not know very well or a smaller network of people with whom you are well acquainted. I consistently teach that your network should be made up primarily of trusted professionals. However, I do think there are certain circumstances in which you may decide to stretch that rule for strategic reasons.

One example is recruiters. Because they are in the "body business," they need sizeable inventories of people with varied backgrounds and strengths; therefore, it makes sense for them to have very large networks. Some have actually acquired 30,000 first-degree connections, which is LinkedIn's upper-end limit. Sales professionals who are responsible for very large territories are another segment of users who many times choose quantity over quality. Personally, now that my book is available in three languages and my LinkedIn consulting business has taken on a more national scope, I have found it beneficial to strategically expand my network as well. You may be in a similar situation that makes you decide to stretch the "trusted professional" rule. My feeling is that as long as you have thoroughly considered your decision, more power to you for using LinkedIn strategically.

When I was a full-time Milwaukee office furniture guy, I would occasionally invite people into my network even though I just met them the previous day at a networking event. This was typically the result of either having had an interesting conversation with the person or having reason to believe further contact with him or her could lead to a mutually beneficial business relationship. Included with these immediate invitations would be a list of times I was available to meet for coffee or lunch so that we could continue to develop our relationship. These are what I call work-in-progress first-degree connections. I would work very hard at building these relationships to a point where I believed the person qualified as a trusted professional.

As mentioned before, the real power of LinkedIn is that it takes connections that are normally invisible and makes them visible. Make your connections visible by transforming your "flat," offline network into a dynamic, multidimensional network of trusted professionals, and you will be on your way to securing that million-workstation project.

APPLYING THE POWER FORMULA

- Your first step is to define what constitutes a trusted professional. I would suggest writing this definition down. These people make up that very important first part of the Power Formula: your **unique relationships.**

- Remember, with each new first-degree connection you add, that person's first-degree connections become new second-degree connections in your network, and their second-degree connections become new third-degree connections in your network. That multiplication process helps you grow your **unique** network exponentially.

CHAPTER 3

Where's the Beef?
The LinkedIn Profile: Basics

Everyone starts on LinkedIn with a profile. A profile can be as simple as your name. However, if you choose to list little but your name, you will be missing a tremendous opportunity to avail yourself of the two major benefits of a LinkedIn profile: the ability to be found and the opportunity to tell your story.

Plain and simple, profiles should be beefy. For those readers who are old enough, think of the Wendy's commercial from the eighties in which the elderly ladies asked "Where's the beef?" as they looked at a tiny hamburger patty dwarfed by a massive bun. For those of you who are not familiar with the commercial, check it out on YouTube. You'll find it quite entertaining.

There are four reasons you want your profile to be beefy:

1. Your LinkedIn profile is a place where you can tell your story completely and fully, so that when people are looking

at your profile, they will be encouraged to do business with you over your competitors. They will see the depth and breadth of your experience, your professional recommendations, and the brands you carry, plus your certifications, educational experience, and all the other qualifications you possess that make you the obvious professional to do business with in the marketplace you serve. I like to refer to a LinkedIn profile as a "resume on steroids."

In contrast to a traditional resume, which is typically a listing of facts and dates, your LinkedIn profile allows you the opportunity to tell your story. It should be a narrative of sorts, where you emphasize your experience and high level of credibility. This "resume on steroids" should shout out "I'm the best at this in my market!"

To help tell your story, you can include details about yourself that, while perhaps bordering on personal information, will get across to the viewer who you are as a unique individual. For example, one of my class attendees told me that through the LinkedIn profile of a prospective client, he learned the guy collected wines—and he also found out which one was his favorite. On the day following his proposal presentation, he followed up with a thank-you note and included a bottle of—you guessed it—his prospective client's favorite wine, and the rest is history. He got the order.

2. Every word in your profile is keyword searchable. Thus, having a beefy profile will increase your chances of being found. As you know from using Google, keyword searching on the Internet is an extremely powerful tool for finding people. Similarly, searching on LinkedIn can produce extremely valuable results. The search function enables you to find people who have certain types of

experience, classifications, and/or brands. In subsequent chapters, I will address in detail how you can increase the likelihood of being found on LinkedIn by strategically including specific information and keywords in the various sections of your profile.

When I owned the office furniture dealership, I was looking for a person interested in bicycling to join a group of cyclists for a charity event my company was sponsoring. Discovering a bicycling enthusiast who happens to be an architect or builder would be a home run. I would then be able to advance a professional relationship, help a charitable organization, *and* enjoy a day of bicycling. Therefore, I searched the words *builder, architect, cycling,* and *bicycling* and instantly had my choice of architects and builders with whom to spend the day. Without those keywords in their profiles, none of these people would have been found. The power of searching is discussed in detail in Chapter 10.

3. A beefy profile shows that you are not a dinosaur. What do I mean by this? For those of us in the Baby Boomer generation, people tend to appreciate the experience we possess, but they are also interested in knowing whether we are keeping abreast of the latest trends in the business world, including social media. A beefy profile will demonstrate you are on top of current trends in your profession or occupation and you embrace technology. You are *not* a dinosaur.

4. You should expect your profile to regularly be compared with those of your competitors. Therefore, in order to gain a competitive advantage, you will want your profile to

include a plethora of information, keywords, and details about who you are, what you hope to accomplish, and how you might be able to assist others.

Many savvy LinkedIn users will review a person's profile before meeting with her for the first time. Personally, I always talk about common interests, mutual friends, or some other interesting fact I found on her profile before I jump into, "So, I hear you need some LinkedIn training." Business professionals use their LinkedIn profiles to tell their stories. As a result, it can be extremely beneficial to review the profile of the potential customer, prospective employee, vendor, or other person with whom you desire to have a business relationship. Because of the vast amount of information available on the Internet in general and on LinkedIn in particular, it has become commonplace to "shop" several vendors online before engaging in direct communication.

Do yourself a favor and take a look at the profiles of some of your competitors. Observe what they are saying about themselves—awards they have won, certifications they hold, types of projects they have worked on, etc.— because this may jog your memory and remind you of similar information you could include in your profile. Based on the information contained in the profiles, would a potential customer be encouraged to do business with you as opposed to one of your competitors? If you think your competitor would get the nod, then start beefing up your profile.

Now that you know the reasons you want your profile to be beefy, the next several chapters will show you the steps to making sure you have all the necessary information on your profile.

APPLYING THE POWER FORMULA

- It will be awfully hard for you to delegate the step of creating a beefy profile to someone else. No one knows your story like you do or can feel as passionate about why that story makes you the best at what you do. That passion will be evident if you personally craft a beefy profile that explains your **unique experience.**

- Try not to turn your profile into a bunch of marketing gobble-dygook. People want to read about what you have done in a simple, understandable format. You need to impress them with what you have accomplished, not with how many buzz-words you can include.

- Start to assemble the details of your **unique experience** by reviewing all of your past jobs and awards, but do not wait to get going on this until you think you have it all together. Subsequent additions to your profile are not only fine but preferable. I will address that topic in more detail later in this book.

Take full advantage of every space on your profile with the help of the handy tip sheet "It's All About Character: Take Full Advantage of Every Space," available on page 193.

CHAPTER 4

Your 10-Second Bumper Sticker
The LinkedIn Profile:
Personal Identification Box

The first item on your LinkedIn profile is what I like to refer to as your "top box" (see Figure 4.1). This box identifies you with several key pieces of information, including your name, photo, headline, location, experience, education, contact info, number of first-degree connections, the first 280 characters of your summary, media you've included in your summary, and your background photo. In this chapter I will address the three most prominent items—name, photo, and headline—because this information is used to identify you throughout the LinkedIn site. Some people will never go to your profile to look at the details, but they will see your personal identification box—what I like to refer to as your "10-second bumper sticker" (see Figure 4.2). Let's address those components one at a time.

Figure 4.1: Your top box is front and center on your profile. Follow my guidelines and make a great first impression.

Figure 4.2: A businesslike photo and compelling headline will help you achieve maximum impact from your 10-second bumper sticker.

Your Name

This element is pretty self-explanatory. Your name should include nothing but your full name, unless you have high-level academic degrees or easily recognizable certifications, such as PhD, MD, CPA, and certain other high-level insurance classifications or nursing classifications, etc. Personally, I wouldn't include designations on the level of an MBA.

Since there will undoubtedly be people who will only know them by their maiden names, some married women who have taken on their husband's last name find it useful to list a maiden name in parentheses—for example, Susan (Jones) Cunningham. You can also list your maiden name, former name, or nickname on your profile by using the Former Name field. To access this, click the pencil to the right of your profile photo and choose *Add former name.* Then choose whether you want this name visible to only your first-level connections, your entire network, or everyone on LinkedIn. Your former name will only appear in LinkedIn searches—not searches done on Internet search engines.

Your Photograph

Most LinkedIn experts are in agreement on the importance of including a photograph in your profile, as well as the benefit of using a headshot (professionally taken or near professional quality) of yourself wearing business attire, smiling, and looking like a person with whom people would want to do business. In fact, LinkedIn suggests you are 21 times more likely to have your profile viewed if you have a photo.

Let's talk about why personal photographs are a hang-up for some people, especially members of the Baby Boomer generation. Plain and simple, we Baby Boomers are afraid to admit that we are in our fifties or sixties. Well, the reality is that you cannot hide behind the computer screen and pretend you are 29 years old forever, and you surely are not going to be able to hide your age when you show up for the job interview or when you show up to collect the check for the order the customer placed after you found him on LinkedIn and put together the sale. So get over it!

Many times people will remember a face before they remember a name. I want to be the person people find on LinkedIn the day after they meet me at an event and say, "I really liked that bald LinkedIn guy. That's the guy. I recognize him by his picture." The person who recognizes you from your photo may be the one who leads you to your million-workstation sale.

Your Headline

A basic headline consists of the company you work for and the position you hold there, but the headline field can contain 120 characters, and it is your opportunity to tell an abbreviated version of your story. In it, you will want to describe your experience and mention how you can help someone who sees your profile or 10-second bumper sticker. You can edit your headline by clicking the pencil icon to the right of your profile photo.

For the first seven or eight months I was on LinkedIn, my headline read, "President and Owner, M&M Office Interiors, where we give you the space you want and the experience you deserve, and LinkedIn trainer." "The space you want and the experience you deserve" is the tagline for the company I owned at the time. I loved my tagline. I paid a lot of money for my tagline. It was the result of very extensive research, and I definitely think it stands for the brand the company has in the marketplace. However, as much as I loved my tagline and what it says, it did not clearly state that my number-one priority was selling office furniture. So I changed my headline to "President, M&M Office Interiors, where we have served the office furniture market for over 50 yrs, and LinkedIn Trainer." It didn't incorporate my business's tagline, but it better described me as a business professional. Unless you work for a multinational corporation that is a household name, you cannot assume the readers of your profile will know what type of products or services you provide. It is imperative for your headline to clearly express what your company does and/or what your business proposition is.

If you have multiple jobs or a primary job and a secondary job, be sure to list all positions you hold. If you are looking for a job, your headline should clearly state that you are a job seeker looking for a position as an IT professional in the food manufacturing/distribution business, for example. If you do not enter a customized headline, LinkedIn will use your most recent job title and company name as your descriptive headline. But do take time to create a powerful headline; it could be the deciding factor in someone's choice to connect with you or look at the details in your full profile.

I personally prefer a narrative-type headline, but a popular alternative is a style that consists of keywords separated by the pipe symbol. To get the pipe symbol, use the shift key together with the backslash key. Some people choose this option because LinkedIn's current search ranking formula gives extra weight to the words in your headline. Because you only have 120 characters available for your headline, using the pipe symbol is a good strategy for putting more keywords in it. I currently have three positions I want to include in my headline, and thus I've found it necessary to switch to using the pipe symbol so that my headline looks like this:

LinkedIn Trainer, Speaker & Consultant | Author, POWER FORMULA FOR LINKEDIN SUCCESS | LinkedIn Expert | Social Selling

Whichever option you choose, include your most important keywords so that when people search for the keywords you included, they will find you—and not your competitor who didn't think to put keywords in his headline.

In summary, I cannot overemphasize the importance of your 10-second bumper sticker. It will travel with you and be your identifier throughout LinkedIn. Be sure it is thorough and correct. If you do not have a photograph or a complete headline, you may cause someone to question your credibility or fail to thoroughly understand your business. As a result, he or she may choose to do business with someone else. Follow the steps I have outlined, and you will be on your way not only to a great 10-second bumper sticker but also to a terrific LinkedIn profile.

APPLYING THE POWER FORMULA

- Your goal with the headline is to create a compelling marketing statement about your **unique experience** in just 120 characters, while also including some critical keywords. Create a few drafts of your statement, and then ask several of your closest connections for a critique of what you have written.

- Do not use an outdated photo of yourself. You are attempting to demonstrate your **unique experience**, and experience comes with age. People need to see you in that photo and put that picture together with the person they just met or are going to meet.

Create a magnetic profile with the help of "Profile Perfection: A Checklist for LinkedIn Optimization," available on page 197.

You only get one chance to make a first impression. To learn how to impress viewers with your LinkedIn headline, download "The Definitive Worksheet to Optimize Your LinkedIn Profile Headline," available at **www.powerformula.net/free**.

CHAPTER 5

Put Your Best Foot Forward

The LinkedIn Profile: Additional Top Box Items

In this chapter I will cover the remaining items included in the top box of your LinkedIn profile. These entries are front and center in an abbreviated form when someone views your profile, and the detail is listed further down on your profile.

Background Photo

Although it's not necessary to have a background photo on your profile, an impressive photo can draw greater attention to your profile. Personally, my custom background photo includes promotional material as well as my contact information (see Figure 5.1), but there are lots of royalty-free stock photos that can look great, too. To add a background photo, click the pencil icon to the right of your profile photo. Next, click the pencil icon at the top right-hand corner of the "Edit intro" box, and then follow the instructions for uploading your photo.

Figure 5.1 An impressive background photo makes for a great first impression.

Your Location

This component of your top box represents the location in which you do business. LinkedIn will automatically assign you a region based on the zip code you provide, but you can choose to insert a different region. For example, if your zip code is 53005, LinkedIn will probably display *Brookfield, Wisconsin*, but you can choose *Greater Milwaukee Area* if you prefer. Because more people will undoubtedly search for professionals in the broader region, you may be presented with more business opportunities if you select *Greater Milwaukee Area*.

If you live in Phoenix but concentrate your business efforts in Los Angeles, it might be advisable to display *Greater Los Angeles Area* on your profile rather than *Greater Phoenix Area*. Then when people do a LinkedIn search for providers of your products or services in Los Angeles, your name will show up in the search results. But let's say you're a job seeker or college student living in Boston and you're looking to relocate to Chicago. Choosing *Greater Chicago Area* as your location could be quite helpful. You are virtually putting yourself in the market where you want to find employment. If you want to take it one step further, you can add a sentence in your Summary section like, *I'm currently attending Boston University, but my goal is to relocate to Chicago for my first professional position.*

Summary Intro

LinkedIn displays (approximately) the first 280 characters of your summary in the top box of your profile. It's important to wisely utilize these characters in order to give readers a sneak peek of what they can expect if they click *Show more* to view your entire summary. In addition, if you'd like to make it easy for people to contact you, include your contact information in these 280 characters (see Figure 5.2). I will provide tips for creating the rest of your summary and adding media to it in a subsequent chapter.

Figure 5.2 Don't make people hunt for your contact info. Put it front and center.

Current Company Name

In your top box, LinkedIn will display the name of the first company listed in your Experience section. However, if you are not currently working there, no company name will be displayed. If you have multiple current jobs, you can rearrange them so your most important job is first, and then that company name will appear in your top box. Do this by holding down the Reorder icon, on the top right of an Experience entry, and dragging it to the position you prefer (see Figure 5.3). In a subsequent chapter, I will discuss other strategies for making the most of your Experience section.

Figure 5.3 The Reorder feature helps you display your most important job in your top box.

Most Recent School Attended

In your top box, LinkedIn will display the name of the first educational institution you have listed in the Education section of your profile. Use the Reorder icon here as well to get your most impressive degree, certification, or other training displayed in your top box. You'll find additional tips for capitalizing on the Education section in the next chapter.

Contact Info

This section is very important but often overlooked. You can add your contact information—including websites, phone, address, e-mail, Twitter, IM, and birthday—by clicking *See contact info* in the top box of your profile and then clicking the pencil icon (see

Figure 5.4). Include whichever ones you use consistently and feel comfortable sharing. Your first-level connections will see all of this information. However, other people will only be able to see your websites and Twitter information.

Figure 5.4: How much contact information you share is up to you.

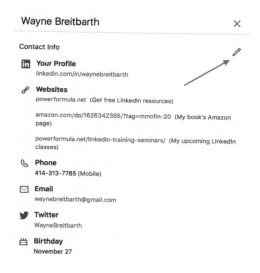

Websites

Included in the Contact Info section is Websites, which contains hyperlinks to specific web pages. People typically have only one thing listed here, most often the website of the company they work for, and the link is usually titled "My Company." Your company's website is a good place to start, but there is a lot of marketing opportunity going to waste if you stop there. You can designate up to three links. Linking enables you to direct people to wherever you would like them to go, giving you the opportunity to send people not only to your company website but also to, for example, a sign-up sheet where they can get on your mailing list. You can link to videos, on YouTube or elsewhere on the web, and you can link to other social media sites like Facebook, your blog, etc. Click the pencil in the Contact Info section to add your websites.

Websites is also a great place to display additional areas of interest, such as organizations and charities in which you are involved, and you will be promoting these organizations' websites by adding them to your profile. You have lots of flexibility here, and you *do not* have to list the URL of your LinkedIn profile as one of the three sites. Using all three for links to other websites will also move your LinkedIn profile up in the search results of sites like Google, Bing, and the other search engines.

Be sure to describe each of these websites. Most people don't realize they have this option and go with the default of "Personal Website," "Company Website," or "Blog." In reality, you can describe your websites with up to thirty characters. Don't miss this opportunity to brand these websites and give one more little marketing push about what you do and what you stand for. You can alter the website's description by selecting *Other* in the pull-down menu and then typing the new description in the box next to the link (see Figure 5.5).

Figure 5.5: Creative website descriptions will encourage readers to take a look at your websites.

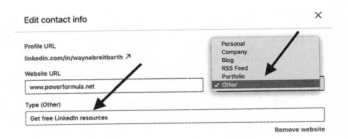

Public Profile URL

When you join LinkedIn, you, in effect, create your own one-page website—your LinkedIn profile—and LinkedIn automatically assigns each new user a somewhat random URL. It includes the user's name and several other seemingly random characters. LinkedIn does, however, allow you to assign your profile a more descriptive URL, and most people choose to simply add their name after www.LinkedIn.com/in/ (see Figure 5.6).

To change your URL, click the words *See contact info* in the right column of your profile. Next, click the blue pencil on the top right and then the blue words below *Profile URL*. After you click the pencil to the right of your current URL, delete the entry in the box and replace it with your full name (no spaces and no capitalization).

I'm lucky to have a unique name that no one had claimed yet, but you may find that your name has been taken. If that's the case, you can add a middle initial or a number following your name in order to save the URL. Changing this address to something closer to your actual name provides a more professional appearance when you use the URL on your resume, letterhead, and/or business card so that people can easily access your profile—your "resume on steroids."

Figure 5.6: A personalized LinkedIn URL will enhance your marketing and branding efforts.

This brings up a point you should understand: When you build a personal LinkedIn profile, you automatically create a public profile, which can be seen by anyone on the Internet who visits your URL. However, you can control exactly how much information is in the public domain, which I refer to as the "Google world," and how much you share only with the LinkedIn community. If you have a photograph on your LinkedIn profile, you can choose to omit the picture from your public profile so that people searching on Google cannot see it. When people are searching on Google or other search engines, your public LinkedIn profile will typically come up on the first page—hopefully it is the very first thing that shows up—but it does not need to have all the same content as your LinkedIn profile. Immediately beneath the place where you created your public profile URL, you can choose what information you'd like to display to the general public by checking or unchecking the boxes (see Figure 5.7).

Figure 5.7: Take control of how much information you share with the general public.

I choose to put everything that I have on my LinkedIn profile on my public profile. I keep my profile very professional, and I want all that information to be in the Google world. That way, if a person is not on LinkedIn, he can still see all the pertinent information about me, all the experiences I have had, the total number of recommendations I have received, and so on. You'll have to decide how much of this information you want to have available in the Google world, and if you stick with a very businesslike LinkedIn profile, you should be able to put almost everything on your public profile as well.

The items that complete your top box—your background photo, location, summary intro, current company name, most recent school attended, and contact info—are crucial to enhancing your credibility and improving the functionality of your LinkedIn profile. It is important to make sure that what's showing up there is exactly what you want people to see. Make a good first impression, stand out from your competitors, and you'll be well on your way to reaching your business and career goals.

APPLYING THE POWER FORMULA

- In your Job Experience and Education sections, it is critical to put your most important current job and education entries at the top of the list so they show up in your top box. Use the Rearrange icon to put your entries in the most favorable order.

- Your current company's website should be your first entry in the Websites section. This will add to the description of your **unique experience**—especially if the website includes customer profiles, a company history, descriptions of what your company does, etc.

Share websites that will generate interest, increase credibility, and provide business leads with the help of the checklist "LinkedIn's Websites Section: Your 'Link' to Future Opportunities," available on page 201.

CHAPTER 6

Resume on Steroids
The LinkedIn Profile:
Experience and Education Sections

As mentioned earlier, I like to think of the LinkedIn profile as a "resume on steroids," and the sections of your profile that most resemble a traditional resume are the Experience and Education sections. You will find these sections in the middle of your profile, and some of the information from these sections is also summarized within the top box.

People often ask me what jobs and educational experiences they should put on their profiles. These are the criteria I suggest you use, not only for jobs and education but also for anything else on your profile:

1. Does putting this on my profile add to my story or increase my credibility?

2. Does putting this on my profile make it easier for people to find me?

3. If I do not put this on my profile and my competitors have it on their profiles, will I be at a competitive disadvantage? In other words, will I be mad I didn't include it on mine?

4. Does this information help people understand what I do and how I can help them?

If the answer to any of these four questions is yes, then, by all means, include that information on your profile.

Experience

My recommendation is to put every job you have ever held on your profile. Begin each job entry with a descriptive title. Take full advantage of the 100 characters LinkedIn allows for the title of each entry in the Experience section. For example, one of my job titles is *CEO | Social Media Trainer and Strategy Consultant (specializing in LinkedIn)*. I could have simply said *CEO*, but this is a much better description of what I do—and the extra keywords (*social media, strategy, consultant, LinkedIn*) will help people find me.

It's important to use plenty of relevant keywords throughout your Experience section. You will also want to highlight not only your present area of expertise but also any specialties relating to previous positions. This is important because when someone searches LinkedIn for a professional with experience in multiple disciplines, the combination of keywords will increase your chances of being found.

It is very important to spend plenty of time crafting the job descriptions on your profile. All too often people fail to spend sufficient time on this because the detail of previous jobs in the

Experience section shows up so far down the page, and they are tired or anxious to move on to other tasks. Do not make this mistake. You never know which job experience or accomplishment will put you ahead of the other candidates in the eyes of a potential customer or employer. And if certain keywords show up multiple times on your profile because you use them in multiple job descriptions, you will be listed higher in the search results, which is definitely a good thing.

Once you've crafted descriptive titles for the positions you've held, describe your jobs in detail—the position you held, what you accomplished, and what experience you gained—and include a list of awards you received while you held each job. You can impress readers further with a timeline of the promotions you received at each job. And if you *really* want to wow them, describe the type of customers or clients you serve(d) and include a killer quote from one of your satisfied customers. The goal here is to add interest and credibility to your story—not simply list your job duties.

When you describe your accomplishments, it's also important to emphasize your diverse experience and ability to complete important tasks. Include any statistics or impressive results you've achieved. Also, highlight experience that aligns with your current and future goals. This will show readers that you are qualified to help them now and in the future.

You will also notice that on my profile I have listed several volunteer positions (see Figure 6.1). Viewers of my profile can see I am actively involved in giving back to my community, and most of us like to hire and work with people who care about others. This is another way to impress viewers of your profile prior to a face-to-face meeting or telephone call. For job seekers, listing volunteer positions and relevant extracurricular experience is a must. For new graduates, where actual job experience may be in short supply, this is your way of showing potential employers that you have been actively involved with specific organizations, worked as part of a team, held leadership positions, and contributed to your community. I prefer to list some of my charitable activities in the Experience section because then they will appear closer to the top of my profile. In Chapter 9 I discuss using an add-on profile section called Volunteer Experience—another great place to list (and promote) your favorite organizations.

Figure 6.1: Improve your credibility by including your volunteer positions.

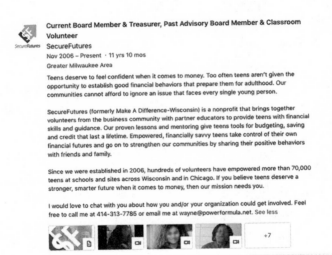

Current Board Member & Treasurer, Past Advisory Board Member & Classroom Volunteer
SecureFutures
Nov 2006 – Present · 11 yrs 10 mos
Greater Milwaukee Area

Teens deserve to feel confident when it comes to money. Too often teens aren't given the opportunity to establish good financial behaviors that prepare them for adulthood. Our communities cannot afford to ignore an issue that faces every single young person.

SecureFutures (formerly Make A Difference-Wisconsin) is a nonprofit that brings together volunteers from the business community with partner educators to provide teens with financial skills and guidance. Our proven lessons and mentoring give teens tools for budgeting, saving and credit that last a lifetime. Empowered, financially savvy teens take control of their own financial futures and go on to strengthen our communities by sharing their positive behaviors with friends and family.

Since we were established in 2006, hundreds of volunteers have empowered more than 70,000 teens at schools and sites across Wisconsin and in Chicago. If you believe teens deserve a stronger, smarter future when it comes to money, then our mission needs you.

I would love to chat with you about how you and/or your organization could get involved. Feel free to call me at 414-313-7785 or email me at wayne@powerformula.net. See less

The Experience section is an extremely important component of your "resume on steroids." It gives you an opportunity to tell the story of who you are as a professional. Spend a significant amount of time writing a detailed description for all jobs listed—and don't forget the keywords. Then step back, review your entries, and ask yourself, *Would I hire me as an employee or vendor?* If the answer is "no," then go back and beef up your job entries.

Education

I recommend that you include all the education you have had, including high school, college, and any significant additional education you received that relates to your industry and/or specialty. One of the benefits of listing all your educational background is that when you are looking to add lots of connections in a hurry—which we will discuss in a subsequent chapter—LinkedIn helps you use the schools or other institutions you attended as a way of finding people with whom you might like to connect.

People sometimes ask me why I would want to list my high school. The first reason is that it can help people find you. The second reason is that people tend to like to do business with fellow alumni, whether they are from high school or college. You cannot predict why a person might select you over your competitors, but a common educational experience could be the deciding factor. So, do yourself a favor and list all schools you have attended.

Under each educational entry, include specific information regarding what your degrees required and what credibility you have because of those degrees. This could include specific classes, internships, leadership roles, study abroad experiences, or anything else you feel shows that your educational experience was more comprehensive than simply completing the coursework required to receive a degree or certification. This is another great way to add credibility to each and every entry on your profile.

You can also list significant industry-specific classes, workshops, or seminars you have attended by clicking the plus sign on the top right of your first Education entry. In the School box, type the name of the school or organization that provided the training or education. When you begin typing the name, LinkedIn will show you a list of all schools that are already in their database. When you choose your school from the list, the school's logo will show up on your profile. You can then type in whatever information about that opportunity you feel will enhance your credibility (see Figure 6.2).

Figure 6.2: Enhance your credibility by highlighting nontraditional educational experiences.

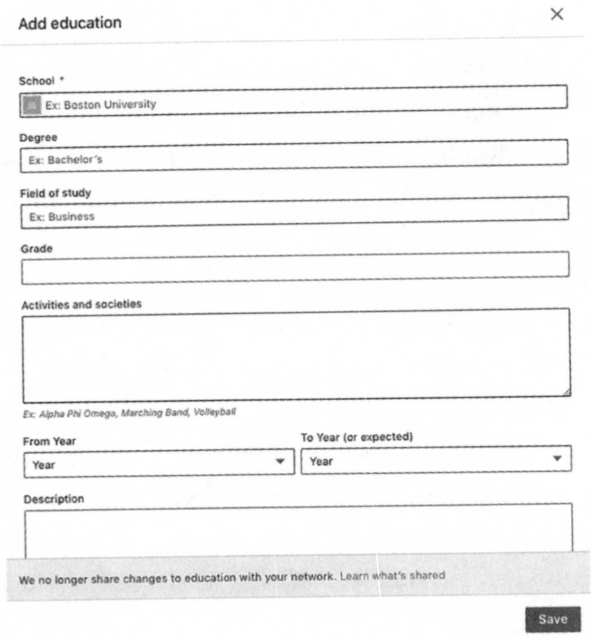

Although the Experience and Education entries look similar to your resume, LinkedIn gives you up to 2,000 characters per entry, which is quite a bit more space to expand on the details of your experience and educational background. This provides a tremendous opportunity to differentiate yourself from other people with similar backgrounds. Impress the people who view these sections of your profile, and it's sure to bring you new business, valuable relationships, or maybe even a terrific new job.

APPLYING THE POWER FORMULA

- In order to be sure each entry you make on your profile thoroughly explains your **unique experience**, try to think of each job as if it were the only one you ever had. This will help you get very detailed in terms of experience, accomplishments, awards, responsibilities, etc. Sometimes we tend to cut corners because, in total, the profile looks fine. However, you never know which of those details presented in a job listing will resonate with the reader of your profile or be the important keywords that help someone find you.

- Do not downplay or forget to include the details of your educational entries; they are an important descriptor of your **unique experience**. With 2,000 characters per job or educational entry, you have a lot of space to use. Remember, integrating keywords into your profile is part of the goal here as well.

- I cannot emphasize enough the importance of including industry-specific workshops, certifications, and training courses as key components of your **unique experience**. It just takes a few moments, and there's a really good chance that your competitors have missed this opportunity, despite the fact that they may have the same experience. This can be a great differentiator.

CHAPTER 7

That's My Boy!

The LinkedIn Profile:
Summary Section

This chapter will concentrate on another important profile section—your summary. I have analyzed thousands of profiles, and I continue to be amazed by how underutilized this section is. It can be extremely powerful in explaining your personal and business brand to viewers of your profile. Also, when filled with the right keywords, it will make it easier for your target audience to find you.

I like to think of this section as your cover letter, because in it you address the reader just as you would in a traditional cover letter. You can also use the summary to direct people to other sections of your profile and emphasize or summarize information you have detailed elsewhere.

To get started, click the pencil icon to the right of your profile photo and scroll down to the Summary section (see Figure 7.1).

Figure 7.1 An impressive Summary section can spark interest in the rest of your profile.

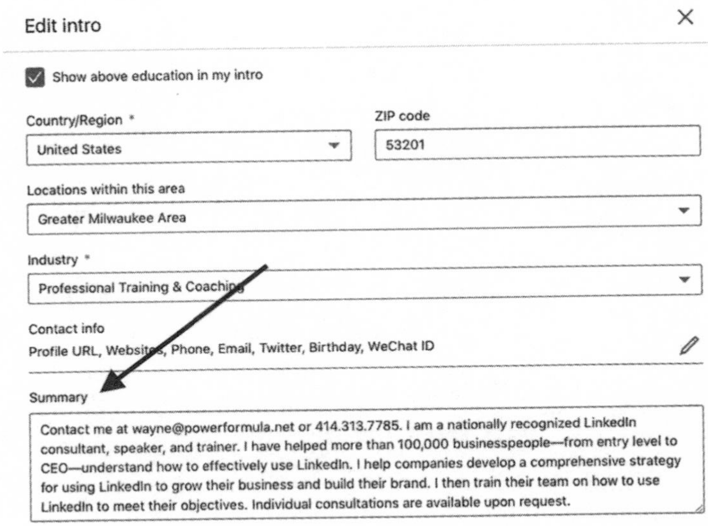

The Summary section can contain up to 2,000 characters, and I recommend taking full advantage of every available character. If you write this section in narrative format, I suggest you use first person, as if you were talking directly to the person reading your profile. Another option is to compose the section in a concise, bulleted format. I prefer the narrative format because it allows you to write as you would speak, giving the section a conversational feel.

If you do write the Summary section in narrative format, consider the specific items you need to cover and the major topics you want to address. You may have several businesses and/or interests you want to highlight in this section of your profile, but this isn't a place to list every detail of every job you've ever had.

Save that information for each respective job description in the Experience section, where you get 2,000 characters for every job. You can summarize some of your work experience in this section, but it is best to use your first paragraph to outline what you are trying to accomplish as a professional, who your perfect customer is, or other information that will help the reader relate to you. After reading the first paragraph of your summary, you want the reader to say, "I'd love to meet this person."

If you are a job seeker, this section should start off with a few sentences outlining the types of jobs that would be a perfect fit for your knowledge and skills. The remainder of the summary should describe why your experience has led you to that conclusion. Include details about how you have saved your previous employers money or increased productivity. You should explain these achievements in the Experience section, but you should also briefly highlight them here as well; some people may not make it down to the detailed job description, and this will be your only chance to tell them about that achievement. If you are a job seeker who is changing career paths, this is the place to explain why you have decided to make a change after years in a different industry or company.

These are some of the topics you may want to include in this section, depending on what your strategy is:

- What makes you, your company, and your products unique
- A description of your perfect customer, vendor relationship, employee, etc.
- A brief summary of the types of job experiences you have had
- Highlights of specific (hopefully quantifiable) things you have accomplished

- An excerpt from a letter of recommendation or testimonial, especially if you have not been able to obtain a LinkedIn recommendation from the person who wrote it
- Some of your hobbies or interests and why they make you a desirable employee or business partner
- Steps the reader can take to get further information on some of your accomplishments, projects you have completed, or awards you have won
- Why you think your experiences make you qualified for this next career step if you're a job seeker
- A brief description of any business relationships that have brought about superior results
- New markets you are considering going into and how viewers of your profile might fit into your plan
- A specific call to action so the reader knows what to do next (see the "Check out my website" section of my profile on page 59)

Here is my LinkedIn summary, which will hopefully demonstrate the concepts discussed:

Contact me at wayne@powerformula.net or 414.313.7785. I am a nationally recognized LinkedIn consultant, speaker, and trainer. I have helped more than 100,000 businesspeople—from entry level to CEO—understand how to effectively use LinkedIn. I help companies develop a comprehensive strategy for using LinkedIn to grow their business and build their brand. I then train their team on how to use LinkedIn to meet their objectives. Individual consultations are available upon request.

I am consistently asked to speak at Executive Agenda (EA), YPO, Vistage and TEC meetings, as well as CEO Roundtables and Renaissance Forums (REF), where my 35+ years of experience as a business owner and manager enables me to help my peers understand how social media can benefit their companies.

My diverse business experience also allows me to share real-life stories and illustrations as I educate, motivate, and entertain audiences at national conventions, industry events, and conferences.

Check out my website at www.powerformula.net, where you can:

- Sign up to receive my FREE weekly social media tips
- Download lots of FREE LinkedIn resources
- View some of my video presentations
- Read my blog
- Learn about the many services I provide for individuals and companies

** I AM NOT ENDORSED BY, CERTIFIED BY, SPONSORED BY, NOR AFFILIATED WITH LINKEDIN CORPORATION IN ANY WAY.

Your Summary section should be written so that if your mother read it, she would say, "That's my boy!" Make sure this "cover letter" section of your profile will be clearly understood by most people and it is not loaded with gobbledygook or jargon. Yes, you still need to be very conscious of the keywords that will put you in the search results you want to be in, but also be sure your story is well told and the reader can clearly see the experiences and accomplishments that got you where you are in your career.

Since LinkedIn does not have a built-in spell-check, write this section in Microsoft Word or another word processor, do a spell-check, count the number of characters (remember, LinkedIn only allows 2,000), and then paste the contents of that document into LinkedIn, confident that your mother will be proud.

Once you have completed your summary, you can add media for visual interest. If you choose the right media, it will add to your credibility and hopefully cause people to engage with you. You will find tips and strategies for adding media in Chapter 9.

You may find it beneficial to review the Summary and Experience sections put forth by some of your competitors. Seeing how they state their business proposition may assist you in thinking about how your business is different from theirs. Remember, none of us has cornered the market on being the only smart guy on LinkedIn. Learn from the profiles of your competitors—that is one of the beauties of LinkedIn.

As I close this chapter, I want to emphasize an important point that applies to your entire profile but tends to crop up most often as people write their own Summary section: You must be willing to brag about yourself when documenting your accomplishments and experiences on your profile. If you have trouble doing this, have someone else help you describe why you are the perfect person for the job or why you should be the vendor of choice. Remember this, too—your competitors will undoubtedly have no trouble bustin' their buttons with pride, so you'd better not be shy about bustin' yours.

APPLYING THE POWER FORMULA

- "Talk to me." That is the phrase I want you to keep top of mind as you write your Summary section. This is one of the few parts of your profile where you have a blank space and no specific boxes to fill in as you share the story of your **unique experience**.

- Take your current marketing materials (brochures, websites, handouts, etc.) and identify all the brands you represent, and include as many as possible in your Summary section.

- If your proposition is **unique**—for example, if you are the only person in your region representing a particular brand—make sure the person viewing your profile knows this by including this information in your Summary section.

- If you have **unique**, important terms that are often misspelled, consider including the misspelled form. That way, when someone searches by that misspelled word, you will still be found.